This journal belongs to:

Please return this journal if you happen to stumble across it. Take it to your local bookstore, at the very least. Surely, they'll be able to get it back to its reader.

A reader should not be without their journal.

The Hodge & Podge Pocket Book Journal is a useful tool for keeping track of the books you read, formatted for small hands and small pockets. Please read and notate sensibly, and always shop at your local indie bookstore.

© 2020 Firebird Creative, LLC.

All rights reserved, which means that no portion of this publication may be reproduced or transmitted, in any form or by any means, without the express written permission of the stakeholders in the Hodge & Podge Library, who are a pair of otters, so you can imagine how that conversation is going to go.

This book was printed in the United States of America. It is a publication of the Hodge & Podge Library, which falls under the aegis of Firebird Creative (Clackamas, OR).

But we don't have pockets, Hodge . . .

www.hodgepodgelibrary.com

POCKET
BOOK
JOURNAL

HODGE & PODGE

This page is blank, which seems like a missed opportunity. Perhaps you can draw pictures of your favorite books. Or maybe scenes of otters, reading your favorite books. Or maybe just otters, busy napping, because they do that a lot too.

POCKET BOOK JOURNAL

[the small hands edition]

TITLE:

AUTHOR:

PUB DATE: **FORMAT:**

PUBLISHER:

WHERE TO SHELVE:

| START: | NOTES |
| FINISH: | |

visual matrix

sexy | smoochy | creepy | scary | literary | explodey | funny | clever | pacing | character | originality | speculative | historic | surprising | comforting | rewarding | verisimilitude | truthiness | oh, it's a hate read | [fill in your own] | [fill in your own] | [fill in your own]

TITLE:

AUTHOR:

PUB DATE: **FORMAT:**

PUBLISHER:

WHERE TO SHELVE:

START: NOTES

FINISH:

---

visual matrix

sexy | smoochy | creepy | scary | literary | explodey | funny | clever | pacing | character | originality | speculative | historic | surprising | comforting | rewarding | verisimilitude | truthiness | oh, it's a hate read | [fill in your own] | [fill in your own] | [fill in your own]

TITLE:

AUTHOR:

PUB DATE:　　　　　**FORMAT:**

PUBLISHER:

WHERE TO SHELVE:

START:	NOTES
FINISH:	

visual matrix

sexy / smoochy / creepy / scary / literary / explodey / funny / clever / pacing / character / originality / speculative / historic / surprising / comforting / rewarding / verisimilitude / truthiness / oh, it's a hate read / [fill in your own] / [fill in your own] / [fill in your own]

TITLE:

AUTHOR:

PUB DATE: **FORMAT:**

PUBLISHER:

WHERE TO SHELVE:

START:	NOTES
FINISH:	

visual matrix

sexy | smoochy | creepy | scary | literary | explodey | funny | clever | pacing | character | originality | speculative | historic | surprising | comforting | rewarding | verisimilitude | truthiness | oh, it's a hate read | [fill in your own] | [fill in your own] | [fill in your own]

10

TITLE:

AUTHOR:

PUB DATE: **FORMAT:**

PUBLISHER:

WHERE TO SHELVE:

START: NOTES

FINISH:

---

visual matrix

- sexy
- smoochy
- creepy
- scary
- literary
- explodey
- funny
- clever
- pacing
- character
- originality
- speculative
- historic
- surprising
- comforting
- rewarding
- verisimilitude
- truthiness
- oh, it's a hate read
- [fill in your own]
- [fill in your own]
- [fill in your own]

TITLE:

AUTHOR:

PUB DATE: **FORMAT:**

PUBLISHER:

WHERE TO SHELVE:

START:	NOTES
FINISH:	

visual matrix

| sexy | smoochy | creepy | scary | literary | explodey | funny | clever | pacing | character | originality | speculative | historic | surprising | comforting | rewarding | verisimilitude | truthiness | oh, it's a hate read | [fill in your own] | [fill in your own] | [fill in your own] |

12

TITLE:

AUTHOR:

PUB DATE: **FORMAT:**

PUBLISHER:

WHERE TO SHELVE:

START: NOTES

FINISH:

---

visual matrix

- sexy
- smoochy
- creepy
- scary
- literary
- explodey
- funny
- clever
- pacing
- character
- originality
- speculative
- historic
- surprising
- comforting
- rewarding
- verisimilitude
- truthiness
- oh, it's a hate read
- [fill in your own]
- [fill in your own]
- [fill in your own]

TITLE:

AUTHOR:

PUB DATE: **FORMAT:**

PUBLISHER:

WHERE TO SHELVE:

START: NOTES

FINISH:

---

visual matrix

| sexy | smoochy | creepy | scary | literary | explodey | funny | clever | pacing | character | originality | speculative | historic | surprising | comforting | rewarding | verisimilitude | truthiness | oh, it's a hate read | [fill in your own] | [fill in your own] | [fill in your own] |

TITLE:

AUTHOR:

PUB DATE: **FORMAT:**

PUBLISHER:

WHERE TO SHELVE:

START: NOTES

FINISH:

visual matrix

| sexy | smoochy | creepy | scary | literary | explodey | funny | clever | pacing | character | originality | speculative | historic | surprising | comforting | rewarding | verisimilitude | truthiness | oh, it's a hate read | [fill in your own] | [fill in your own] | [fill in your own] |

15

TITLE:

AUTHOR:

PUB DATE: **FORMAT:**

PUBLISHER:

WHERE TO SHELVE:

| **START:** | NOTES |
| **FINISH:** | |

visual matrix

sexy | smoochy | creepy | scary | literary | explodey | funny | clever | pacing | character | originality | speculative | historic | surprising | comforting | rewarding | verisimilitude | truthiness | oh, it's a hate read | [fill in your own] | [fill in your own] | [fill in your own]

16

TITLE:

AUTHOR:

PUB DATE: **FORMAT:**

PUBLISHER:

WHERE TO SHELVE:

START:	NOTES
FINISH:	

visual matrix

sexy / smoochy / creepy / scary / literary / explodey / funny / clever / pacing / character / originality / speculative / historic / surprising / comforting / rewarding / verisimilitude / truthiness / oh, it's a hate read / [fill in your own] / [fill in your own] / [fill in your own]

TITLE:

AUTHOR:

PUB DATE: **FORMAT:**

PUBLISHER:

WHERE TO SHELVE:

START:	NOTES
FINISH:	

visual matrix

sexy | smoochy | creepy | scary | literary | explodey | funny | clever | pacing | character | originality | speculative | historic | surprising | comforting | rewarding | verisimilitude | truthiness | oh, it's a hate read | [fill in your own] | [fill in your own] | [fill in your own]

18

TITLE:

AUTHOR:

PUB DATE: **FORMAT:**

PUBLISHER:

WHERE TO SHELVE:

START:	NOTES
FINISH:	

visual matrix

sexy / smoochy / creepy / scary / literary / explodey / funny / clever / pacing / character / originality / speculative / historic / surprising / comforting / rewarding / verisimilitude / truthiness / oh, it's a hate read / [fill in your own] / [fill in your own] / [fill in your own]

TITLE:

AUTHOR:

PUB DATE: **FORMAT:**

PUBLISHER:

WHERE TO SHELVE:

START: NOTES

FINISH:

---

visual matrix

| sexy | smoochy | creepy | scary | literary | explodey | funny | clever | pacing | character | originality | speculative | historic | surprising | comforting | rewarding | verisimilitude | truthiness | oh, it's a hate read | [fill in your own] | [fill in your own] | [fill in your own] |

TITLE:

AUTHOR:

PUB DATE: **FORMAT:**

PUBLISHER:

WHERE TO SHELVE:

START: NOTES

FINISH:

---

visual matrix

| sexy | smoochy | creepy | scary | literary | explodey | funny | clever | pacing | character | originality | speculative | historic | surprising | comforting | rewarding | verisimilitude | truthiness | oh, it's a hate read | [fill in your own] | [fill in your own] | [fill in your own] |

TITLE:

AUTHOR:

PUB DATE: **FORMAT:**

PUBLISHER:

WHERE TO SHELVE:

START:	NOTES
FINISH:	

visual matrix

sexy · smoochy · creepy · scary · literary · explodey · funny · clever · pacing · character · originality · speculative · historic · surprising · comforting · rewarding · verisimilitude · truthiness · oh, it's a hate read · [fill in your own] · [fill in your own] · [fill in your own]

22

TITLE:

AUTHOR:

PUB DATE: **FORMAT:**

PUBLISHER:

WHERE TO SHELVE:

START: NOTES

FINISH:

---

visual matrix

sexy · smoochy · creepy · scary · literary · explodey · funny · clever · pacing · character · originality · speculative · historic · surprising · comforting · rewarding · verisimilitude · truthiness · oh, it's a hate read · [fill in your own] · [fill in your own] · [fill in your own]

TITLE:

AUTHOR:

PUB DATE: **FORMAT:**

PUBLISHER:

WHERE TO SHELVE:

START:	NOTES
FINISH:	

visual matrix

- sexy
- smoochy
- creepy
- scary
- literary
- explodey
- funny
- clever
- pacing
- character
- originality
- speculative
- historic
- surprising
- comforting
- rewarding
- verisimilitude
- truthiness
- oh, it's a hate read
- [fill in your own]
- [fill in your own]
- [fill in your own]

TITLE:

AUTHOR:

PUB DATE: **FORMAT:**

PUBLISHER:

WHERE TO SHELVE:

| **START:** | NOTES |
| **FINISH:** | |

visual matrix

sexy / smoochy / creepy / scary / literary / explodey / funny / clever / pacing / character / originality / speculative / historic / surprising / comforting / rewarding / verisimilitude / truthiness / oh, it's a hate read / [fill in your own] / [fill in your own] / [fill in your own]

TITLE:

AUTHOR:

PUB DATE: **FORMAT:**

PUBLISHER:

WHERE TO SHELVE:

START:	NOTES
FINISH:	

visual matrix

sexy | smoochy | creepy | scary | literary | explodey | funny | clever | pacing | character | originality | speculative | historic | surprising | comforting | rewarding | verisimilitude | truthiness | oh, it's a hate read | [fill in your own] | [fill in your own] | [fill in your own]

26

TITLE:

AUTHOR:

PUB DATE: **FORMAT:**

PUBLISHER:

WHERE TO SHELVE:

START: NOTES

FINISH:

---

visual matrix

sexy / smoochy / creepy / scary / literary / explodey / funny / clever / pacing / character / originality / speculative / historic / surprising / comforting / rewarding / verisimilitude / truthiness / oh, it's a hate read / [fill in your own] / [fill in your own] / [fill in your own]

TITLE:

AUTHOR:

PUB DATE: **FORMAT:**

PUBLISHER:

WHERE TO SHELVE:

START:	NOTES
FINISH:	

visual matrix

sexy | smoochy | creepy | scary | literary | explodey | funny | clever | pacing | character | originality | speculative | historic | surprising | comforting | rewarding | verisimilitude | truthiness | oh, it's a hate read | [fill in your own] | [fill in your own] | [fill in your own]

28

TITLE:

AUTHOR:

PUB DATE: **FORMAT:**

PUBLISHER:

WHERE TO SHELVE:

START:	NOTES
FINISH:	

visual matrix

sexy | smoochy | creepy | scary | literary | explodey | funny | clever | pacing | character | originality | speculative | historic | surprising | comforting | rewarding | verisimilitude | truthiness | oh, it's a hate read | [fill in your own] | [fill in your own] | [fill in your own]

TITLE:

AUTHOR:

PUB DATE: **FORMAT:**

PUBLISHER:

WHERE TO SHELVE:

START:	NOTES
FINISH:	

visual matrix

sexy | smoochy | creepy | scary | literary | explodey | funny | clever | pacing | character | originality | speculative | historic | surprising | comforting | rewarding | verisimilitude | truthiness | oh, it's a hate read | [fill in your own] | [fill in your own] | [fill in your own]

30

TITLE:

AUTHOR:

PUB DATE: **FORMAT:**

PUBLISHER:

WHERE TO SHELVE:

START:	NOTES
FINISH:	

visual matrix

sexy / smoochy / creepy / scary / literary / explodey / funny / clever / pacing / character / originality / speculative / historic / surprising / comforting / rewarding / verisimilitude / truthiness / oh, it's a hate read / [fill in your own] / [fill in your own] / [fill in your own]

31

TITLE:

AUTHOR:

PUB DATE: **FORMAT:**

PUBLISHER:

WHERE TO SHELVE:

START:	NOTES
FINISH:	

visual matrix

sexy | smoochy | creepy | scary | literary | explodey | funny | clever | pacing | character | originality | speculative | historic | surprising | comforting | rewarding | verisimilitude | truthiness | oh, it's a hate read | [fill in your own] | [fill in your own] | [fill in your own]

32

TITLE:

AUTHOR:

PUB DATE: **FORMAT:**

PUBLISHER:

WHERE TO SHELVE:

START:	NOTES
FINISH:	

visual matrix

sexy / smoochy / creepy / scary / literary / explodey / funny / clever / pacing / character / originality / speculative / historic / surprising / comforting / rewarding / verisimilitude / truthiness / oh, it's a hate read / [fill in your own] / [fill in your own] / [fill in your own]

TITLE:

AUTHOR:

PUB DATE: **FORMAT:**

PUBLISHER:

WHERE TO SHELVE:

START:	NOTES
FINISH:	

visual matrix

sexy | smoochy | creepy | scary | literary | explodey | funny | clever | pacing | character | originality | speculative | historic | surprising | comforting | rewarding | verisimilitude | truthiness | oh, it's a hate read | [fill in your own] | [fill in your own] | [fill in your own]

34

TITLE: ....

AUTHOR: ....

PUB DATE: .... **FORMAT:** ....

PUBLISHER: ....

WHERE TO SHELVE:

START:	NOTES
FINISH:	

visual matrix

sexy · smoochy · creepy · scary · literary · explodey · funny · clever · pacing · character · originality · speculative · historic · surprising · comforting · rewarding · verisimilitude · truthiness · oh, it's a hate read · [fill in your own] · [fill in your own] · [fill in your own]

35

TITLE:

AUTHOR:

PUB DATE: **FORMAT:**

PUBLISHER:

WHERE TO SHELVE:

START:	NOTES
FINISH:	

visual matrix

sexy | smoochy | creepy | scary | literary | explodey | funny | clever | pacing | character | originality | speculative | historic | surprising | comforting | rewarding | verisimilitude | truthiness | oh, it's a hate read | [fill in your own] | [fill in your own] | [fill in your own]

36

TITLE:

AUTHOR:

PUB DATE: **FORMAT:**

PUBLISHER:

WHERE TO SHELVE:

START: NOTES

FINISH:

---

visual matrix

| sexy | smoochy | creepy | scary | literary | explodey | funny | clever | pacing | character | originality | speculative | historic | surprising | comforting | rewarding | verisimilitude | truthiness | oh, it's a hate read | [fill in your own] | [fill in your own] | [fill in your own] |

37

TITLE:

AUTHOR:

PUB DATE: **FORMAT:**

PUBLISHER:

WHERE TO SHELVE:

| **START:** | NOTES |
| **FINISH:** | |

visual matrix

sexy | smoochy | creepy | scary | literary | explodey | funny | clever | pacing | character | originality | speculative | historic | surprising | comforting | rewarding | verisimilitude | truthiness | oh, it's a hate read | [fill in your own] | [fill in your own] | [fill in your own]

38

TITLE:

AUTHOR:

PUB DATE: **FORMAT:**

PUBLISHER:

WHERE TO SHELVE:

| **START:** | NOTES |
| **FINISH:** | |

visual matrix

| sexy | smoochy | creepy | scary | literary | explodey | funny | clever | pacing | character | originality | speculative | historic | surprising | comforting | rewarding | verisimilitude | truthiness | oh, it's a hate read | [fill in your own] | [fill in your own] | [fill in your own] |

TITLE:

AUTHOR:

PUB DATE: **FORMAT:**

PUBLISHER:

WHERE TO SHELVE:

START:	NOTES
FINISH:	

visual matrix

sexy / smoochy / creepy / scary / literary / explodey / funny / clever / pacing / character / originality / speculative / historic / surprising / comforting / rewarding / verisimilitude / truthiness / oh, it's a hate read / [fill in your own] / [fill in your own] / [fill in your own]

40

TITLE:

AUTHOR:

PUB DATE: **FORMAT:**

PUBLISHER:

WHERE TO SHELVE:

START:	NOTES
FINISH:	

visual matrix

sexy / smoochy / creepy / scary / literary / explodey / funny / clever / pacing / character / originality / speculative / historic / surprising / comforting / rewarding / verisimilitude / truthiness / oh, it's a hate read / [fill in your own] / [fill in your own] / [fill in your own]

41

TITLE:

AUTHOR:

PUB DATE: **FORMAT:**

PUBLISHER:

WHERE TO SHELVE:

| **START:** | NOTES |
| **FINISH:** | |

visual matrix

sexy | smoochy | creepy | scary | literary | explodey | funny | clever | pacing | character | originality | speculative | historic | surprising | comforting | rewarding | verisimilitude | truthiness | oh, it's a hate read | [fill in your own] | [fill in your own] | [fill in your own]

42

TITLE:

AUTHOR:

PUB DATE: **FORMAT:**

PUBLISHER:

WHERE TO SHELVE:

START:	NOTES
FINISH:	

visual matrix

sexy / smoochy / creepy / scary / literary / explodey / funny / clever / pacing / character / originality / speculative / historic / surprising / comforting / rewarding / verisimilitude / truthiness / oh, it's a hate read / [fill in your own] / [fill in your own] / [fill in your own]

43

TITLE:

AUTHOR:

PUB DATE: **FORMAT:**

PUBLISHER:

WHERE TO SHELVE:

START:	NOTES
FINISH:	

visual matrix

sexy | smoochy | creepy | scary | literary | explodey | funny | clever | pacing | character | originality | speculative | historic | surprising | comforting | rewarding | verisimilitude | truthiness | oh, it's a hate read | [fill in your own] | [fill in your own] | [fill in your own]

44

TITLE:

AUTHOR:

PUB DATE: **FORMAT:**

PUBLISHER:

WHERE TO SHELVE:

START:	NOTES
FINISH:	

visual matrix

sexy / smoochy / creepy / scary / literary / explodey / funny / clever / pacing / character / originality / speculative / historic / surprising / comforting / rewarding / verisimilitude / truthiness / oh, it's a hate read / [fill in your own] / [fill in your own] / [fill in your own]

TITLE:

AUTHOR:

PUB DATE: **FORMAT:**

PUBLISHER:

WHERE TO SHELVE:

START:	NOTES
FINISH:	

visual matrix

sexy | smoochy | creepy | scary | literary | explodey | funny | clever | pacing | character | originality | speculative | historic | surprising | comforting | rewarding | verisimilitude | truthiness | oh, it's a hate read | [fill in your own] | [fill in your own] | [fill in your own]

TITLE:

AUTHOR:

PUB DATE: **FORMAT:**

PUBLISHER:

WHERE TO SHELVE:

START: NOTES

FINISH:

---

visual matrix

| sexy | smoochy | creepy | scary | literary | explodey | funny | clever | pacing | character | originality | speculative | historic | surprising | comforting | rewarding | verisimilitude | truthiness | oh, it's a hate read | [fill in your own] | [fill in your own] | [fill in your own] |

47

TITLE:
....

AUTHOR:
....

PUB DATE: .... **FORMAT:** ....

PUBLISHER:
....

WHERE TO SHELVE:

START:	**NOTES**
FINISH:	

visual matrix

| sexy | smoochy | creepy | scary | literary | explodey | funny | clever | pacing | character | originality | speculative | historic | surprising | comforting | rewarding | verisimilitude | truthiness | oh, it's a hate read | [fill in your own] | [fill in your own] | [fill in your own] |

48

TITLE:

AUTHOR:

PUB DATE: **FORMAT:**

PUBLISHER:

WHERE TO SHELVE:

START:	NOTES
FINISH:	

visual matrix

sexy / smoochy / creepy / scary / literary / explodey / funny / clever / pacing / character / originality / speculative / historic / surprising / comforting / rewarding / verisimilitude / truthiness / oh, it's a hate read / [fill in your own] / [fill in your own] / [fill in your own]

TITLE:

AUTHOR:

PUB DATE: **FORMAT:**

PUBLISHER:

WHERE TO SHELVE:

START:	NOTES
FINISH:	

visual matrix

sexy · smoochy · creepy · scary · literary · explodey · funny · clever · pacing · character · originality · speculative · historic · surprising · comforting · rewarding · verisimilitude · truthiness · oh, it's a hate read · [fill in your own] · [fill in your own] · [fill in your own]

50

TITLE:

AUTHOR:

PUB DATE: **FORMAT:**

PUBLISHER:

WHERE TO SHELVE:

START: NOTES

FINISH:

---

visual matrix

- sexy
- smoochy
- creepy
- scary
- literary
- explodey
- funny
- clever
- pacing
- character
- originality
- speculative
- historic
- surprising
- comforting
- rewarding
- verisimilitude
- truthiness
- oh, it's a hate read
- [fill in your own]
- [fill in your own]
- [fill in your own]

51

TITLE:

AUTHOR:

PUB DATE: **FORMAT:**

PUBLISHER:

WHERE TO SHELVE:

START:	NOTES
FINISH:	

visual matrix

sexy / smoochy / creepy / scary / literary / explodey / funny / clever / pacing / character / originality / speculative / historic / surprising / comforting / rewarding / verisimilitude / truthiness / oh, it's a hate read / [fill in your own] / [fill in your own] / [fill in your own]

52

TITLE:

AUTHOR:

PUB DATE: **FORMAT:**

PUBLISHER:

WHERE TO SHELVE:

| START: | NOTES |
| FINISH: | |

visual matrix

| sexy | smoochy | creepy | scary | literary | explodey | funny | clever | pacing | character | originality | speculative | historic | surprising | comforting | rewarding | verisimilitude | truthiness | oh, it's a hate read | [fill in your own] | [fill in your own] | [fill in your own] |

53

TITLE:

AUTHOR:

PUB DATE: **FORMAT:**

PUBLISHER:

WHERE TO SHELVE:

START: NOTES

FINISH:

---

visual matrix

sexy | smoochy | creepy | scary | literary | explodey | funny | clever | pacing | character | originality | speculative | historic | surprising | comforting | rewarding | verisimilitude | truthiness | oh, it's a hate read | [fill in your own] | [fill in your own] | [fill in your own]

54

TITLE:

AUTHOR:

PUB DATE: **FORMAT:**

PUBLISHER:

WHERE TO SHELVE:

START:	NOTES
FINISH:	

visual matrix

sexy / smoochy / creepy / scary / literary / explodey / funny / clever / pacing / character / originality / speculative / historic / surprising / comforting / rewarding / verisimilitude / truthiness / oh, it's a hate read / [fill in your own] / [fill in your own] / [fill in your own]

TITLE:

AUTHOR:

PUB DATE: **FORMAT:**

PUBLISHER:

WHERE TO SHELVE:

START:	NOTES
FINISH:	

visual matrix

sexy | smoochy | creepy | scary | literary | explodey | funny | clever | pacing | character | originality | speculative | historic | surprising | comforting | rewarding | verisimilitude | truthiness | oh, it's a hate read | [fill in your own] | [fill in your own] | [fill in your own]

TITLE:

AUTHOR:

PUB DATE: **FORMAT:**

PUBLISHER:

WHERE TO SHELVE:

START:	NOTES
FINISH:	

visual matrix

sexy · smoochy · creepy · scary · literary · explodey · funny · clever · pacing · character · originality · speculative · historic · surprising · comforting · rewarding · verisimilitude · truthiness · oh, it's a hate read · [fill in your own] · [fill in your own] · [fill in your own]

57

TITLE:

AUTHOR:

PUB DATE: **FORMAT:**

PUBLISHER:

WHERE TO SHELVE:

START:	NOTES
FINISH:	

visual matrix

sexy / smoochy / creepy / scary / literary / explodey / funny / clever / pacing / character / originality / speculative / historic / surprising / comforting / rewarding / verisimilitude / truthiness / oh, it's a hate read / [fill in your own] / [fill in your own] / [fill in your own]

TITLE:

AUTHOR:

PUB DATE: **FORMAT:**

PUBLISHER:

WHERE TO SHELVE:

START:	NOTES
FINISH:	

visual matrix

sexy | smoochy | creepy | scary | literary | explodey | funny | clever | pacing | character | originality | speculative | historic | surprising | comforting | rewarding | verisimilitude | truthiness | oh, it's a hate read | [fill in your own] | [fill in your own] | [fill in your own]

TITLE:

AUTHOR:

PUB DATE: **FORMAT:**

PUBLISHER:

WHERE TO SHELVE:

START:	NOTES
FINISH:	

visual matrix

- sexy
- smoochy
- creepy
- scary
- literary
- explodey
- funny
- clever
- pacing
- character
- originality
- speculative
- historic
- surprising
- comforting
- rewarding
- verisimilitude
- truthiness
- oh, it's a hate read
- [fill in your own]
- [fill in your own]
- [fill in your own]

60

TITLE:

AUTHOR:

PUB DATE: **FORMAT:**

PUBLISHER:

WHERE TO SHELVE:

| **START:** | NOTES |
| **FINISH:** | |

visual matrix

sexy / smoochy / creepy / scary / literary / explodey / funny / clever / pacing / character / originality / speculative / historic / surprising / comforting / rewarding / verisimilitude / truthiness / oh, it's a hate read / [fill in your own] / [fill in your own] / [fill in your own]

61

TITLE:

AUTHOR:

PUB DATE: **FORMAT:**

PUBLISHER:

WHERE TO SHELVE:

| **START:** | NOTES |
| **FINISH:** | |

visual matrix

sexy · smoochy · creepy · scary · literary · explodey · funny · clever · pacing · character · originality · speculative · historic · surprising · comforting · rewarding · verisimilitude · truthiness · oh, it's a hate read · [fill in your own] · [fill in your own] · [fill in your own]

TITLE:

AUTHOR:

PUB DATE: **FORMAT:**

PUBLISHER:

WHERE TO SHELVE:

| **START:** | NOTES |
| **FINISH:** | |

visual matrix

sexy | smoochy | creepy | scary | literary | explodey | funny | clever | pacing | character | originality | speculative | historic | surprising | comforting | rewarding | verisimilitude | truthiness | oh, it's a hate read | [fill in your own] | [fill in your own] | [fill in your own]

63

TITLE:

AUTHOR:

PUB DATE: **FORMAT:**

PUBLISHER:

WHERE TO SHELVE:

| **START:** | NOTES |
| **FINISH:** | |

visual matrix

sexy | smoochy | creepy | scary | literary | explodey | funny | clever | pacing | character | originality | speculative | historic | surprising | comforting | rewarding | verisimilitude | truthiness | oh, it's a hate read | [fill in your own] | [fill in your own] | [fill in your own]

64

TITLE:

AUTHOR:

PUB DATE: **FORMAT:**

PUBLISHER:

WHERE TO SHELVE:

START:	NOTES
FINISH:	

visual matrix

sexy · smoochy · creepy · scary · literary · explodey · funny · clever · pacing · character · originality · speculative · historic · surprising · comforting · rewarding · verisimilitude · truthiness · oh, it's a hate read · [fill in your own] · [fill in your own] · [fill in your own]

TITLE:

AUTHOR:

PUB DATE: **FORMAT:**

PUBLISHER:

WHERE TO SHELVE:

START:	NOTES
FINISH:	

visual matrix

sexy / smoochy / creepy / scary / literary / explodey / funny / clever / pacing / character / originality / speculative / historic / surprising / comforting / rewarding / verisimilitude / truthiness / oh, it's a hate read / [fill in your own] / [fill in your own] / [fill in your own]

TITLE:

AUTHOR:

PUB DATE: **FORMAT:**

PUBLISHER:

WHERE TO SHELVE:

START: NOTES

FINISH:

---

visual matrix

| sexy | smoochy | creepy | scary | literary | explodey | funny | clever | pacing | character | originality | speculative | historic | surprising | comforting | rewarding | verisimilitude | truthiness | oh, it's a hate read | [fill in your own] | [fill in your own] | [fill in your own] |

TITLE:

AUTHOR:

PUB DATE: **FORMAT:**

PUBLISHER:

WHERE TO SHELVE:

START: NOTES

FINISH:

---

visual matrix

sexy | smoochy | creepy | scary | literary | explodey | funny | clever | pacing | character | originality | speculative | historic | surprising | comforting | rewarding | verisimilitude | truthiness | oh, it's a hate read | [fill in your own] | [fill in your own] | [fill in your own]

68

TITLE:

AUTHOR:

PUB DATE: **FORMAT:**

PUBLISHER:

WHERE TO SHELVE:

START:	NOTES
FINISH:	

visual matrix

sexy | smoochy | creepy | scary | literary | explodey | funny | clever | pacing | character | originality | speculative | historic | surprising | comforting | rewarding | verisimilitude | truthiness | oh, it's a hate read | [fill in your own] | [fill in your own] | [fill in your own]

TITLE:

AUTHOR:

PUB DATE: **FORMAT:**

PUBLISHER:

WHERE TO SHELVE:

START:	NOTES
FINISH:	

visual matrix

sexy | smoochy | creepy | scary | literary | explodey | funny | clever | pacing | character | originality | speculative | historic | surprising | comforting | rewarding | verisimilitude | truthiness | oh, it's a hate read | [fill in your own] | [fill in your own] | [fill in your own]

TITLE:

AUTHOR:

PUB DATE: **FORMAT:**

PUBLISHER:

WHERE TO SHELVE:

START:	NOTES
FINISH:	

visual matrix

sexy / smoochy / creepy / scary / literary / explodey / funny / clever / pacing / character / originality / speculative / historic / surprising / comforting / rewarding / verisimilitude / truthiness / oh, it's a hate read / [fill in your own] / [fill in your own] / [fill in your own]

TITLE:

AUTHOR:

PUB DATE: **FORMAT:**

PUBLISHER:

WHERE TO SHELVE:

START:	NOTES
FINISH:	

visual matrix

sexy / smoochy / creepy / scary / literary / explodey / funny / clever / pacing / character / originality / speculative / historic / surprising / comforting / rewarding / verisimilitude / truthiness / oh, it's a hate read / [fill in your own] / [fill in your own] / [fill in your own]

72

TITLE:

AUTHOR:

PUB DATE: **FORMAT:**

PUBLISHER:

WHERE TO SHELVE:

START:	NOTES
FINISH:	

visual matrix

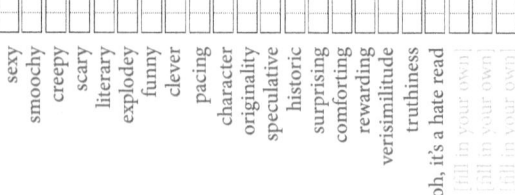

sexy · smoochy · creepy · scary · literary · explodey · funny · clever · pacing · character · originality · speculative · historic · surprising · comforting · rewarding · verisimilitude · truthiness · oh, it's a hate read · [fill in your own] · [fill in your own] · [fill in your own]

73

TITLE:

AUTHOR:

PUB DATE: **FORMAT:**

PUBLISHER:

WHERE TO SHELVE:

START:	NOTES
FINISH:	

visual matrix

sexy | smoochy | creepy | scary | literary | explodey | funny | clever | pacing | character | originality | speculative | historic | surprising | comforting | rewarding | verisimilitude | truthiness | oh, it's a hate read | [fill in your own] | [fill in your own] | [fill in your own]

74

TITLE:

AUTHOR:

PUB DATE: **FORMAT:**

PUBLISHER:

WHERE TO SHELVE:

START: NOTES

FINISH:

visual matrix

sexy | smoochy | creepy | scary | literary | explodey | funny | clever | pacing | character | originality | speculative | historic | surprising | comforting | rewarding | verisimilitude | truthiness | oh, it's a hate read | [fill in your own] | [fill in your own] | [fill in your own]

TITLE:

AUTHOR:

PUB DATE: **FORMAT:**

PUBLISHER:

WHERE TO SHELVE:

START:	NOTES
FINISH:	

visual matrix

sexy / smoochy / creepy / scary / literary / explodey / funny / clever / pacing / character / originality / speculative / historic / surprising / comforting / rewarding / verisimilitude / truthiness / oh, it's a hate read / [fill in your own] / [fill in your own] / [fill in your own]

TITLE:

AUTHOR:

PUB DATE: **FORMAT:**

PUBLISHER:

WHERE TO SHELVE:

START:	NOTES
FINISH:	

visual matrix

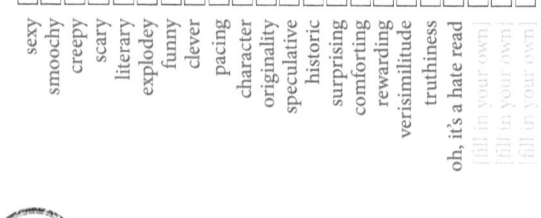

sexy, smoochy, creepy, scary, literary, explodey, funny, clever, pacing, character, originality, speculative, historic, surprising, comforting, rewarding, verisimilitude, truthiness, oh, it's a hate read, [fill in your own], [fill in your own], [fill in your own]

TITLE:

AUTHOR:

PUB DATE: **FORMAT:**

PUBLISHER:

WHERE TO SHELVE:

START:	NOTES
FINISH:	

visual matrix

| sexy | smoochy | creepy | scary | literary | explodey | funny | clever | pacing | character | originality | speculative | historic | surprising | comforting | rewarding | verisimilitude | truthiness | oh, it's a hate read | [fill in your own] | [fill in your own] | [fill in your own] |

TITLE:

AUTHOR:

PUB DATE: **FORMAT:**

PUBLISHER:

WHERE TO SHELVE:

| **START:** | **NOTES** |
| **FINISH:** | |

visual matrix

sexy | smoochy | creepy | scary | literary | explodey | funny | clever | pacing | character | originality | speculative | historic | surprising | comforting | rewarding | verisimilitude | truthiness | oh, it's a hate read | [fill in your own] | [fill in your own] | [fill in your own]

TITLE:

AUTHOR:

PUB DATE: **FORMAT:**

PUBLISHER:

WHERE TO SHELVE:

START:	NOTES
FINISH:	

visual matrix

sexy | smoochy | creepy | scary | literary | explodey | funny | clever | pacing | character | originality | speculative | historic | surprising | comforting | rewarding | verisimilitude | truthiness | oh, it's a hate read | [fill in your own] | [fill in your own] | [fill in your own]

80

TITLE:

AUTHOR:

PUB DATE: **FORMAT:**

PUBLISHER:

WHERE TO SHELVE:

| **START:** | NOTES |
| **FINISH:** | |

visual matrix

sexy / smoochy / creepy / scary / literary / explodey / funny / clever / pacing / character / originality / speculative / historic / surprising / comforting / rewarding / verisimilitude / truthiness / oh, it's a hate read / [fill in your own] / [fill in your own] / [fill in your own]

TITLE:

AUTHOR:

PUB DATE: **FORMAT:**

PUBLISHER:

WHERE TO SHELVE:

START:	NOTES
FINISH:	

visual matrix

sexy | smoochy | creepy | scary | literary | explodey | funny | clever | pacing | character | originality | speculative | historic | surprising | comforting | rewarding | verisimilitude | truthiness | oh, it's a hate read | [fill in your own] | [fill in your own] | [fill in your own]

82

TITLE:

AUTHOR:

PUB DATE: **FORMAT:**

PUBLISHER:

WHERE TO SHELVE:

START: NOTES

FINISH:

---

visual matrix

sexy | smoochy | creepy | scary | literary | explodey | funny | clever | pacing | character | originality | speculative | historic | surprising | comforting | rewarding | verisimilitude | truthiness | oh, it's a hate read | [fill in your own] | [fill in your own] | [fill in your own]

TITLE:

AUTHOR:

PUB DATE: **FORMAT:**

PUBLISHER:

WHERE TO SHELVE:

START: NOTES

FINISH:

---

visual matrix

sexy | smoochy | creepy | scary | literary | explodey | funny | clever | pacing | character | originality | speculative | historic | surprising | comforting | rewarding | verisimilitude | truthiness | oh, it's a hate read | [fill in your own] | [fill in your own] | [fill in your own]

TITLE:

AUTHOR:

PUB DATE: **FORMAT:**

PUBLISHER:

WHERE TO SHELVE:

START:	NOTES
FINISH:	

visual matrix

sexy / smoochy / creepy / scary / literary / explodey / funny / clever / pacing / character / originality / speculative / historic / surprising / comforting / rewarding / verisimilitude / truthiness / oh, it's a hate read / [fill in your own] / [fill in your own] / [fill in your own]

85

TITLE:

AUTHOR:

PUB DATE: **FORMAT:**

PUBLISHER:

WHERE TO SHELVE:

START: NOTES

FINISH:

---

visual matrix

sexy | smoochy | creepy | scary | literary | explodey | funny | clever | pacing | character | originality | speculative | historic | surprising | comforting | rewarding | verisimilitude | truthiness | oh, it's a hate read | [fill in your own] | [fill in your own] | [fill in your own]

86

TITLE:

AUTHOR:

PUB DATE: **FORMAT:**

PUBLISHER:

WHERE TO SHELVE:

START: NOTES

FINISH:

---

visual matrix

sexy | smoochy | creepy | scary | literary | explodey | funny | clever | pacing | character | originality | speculative | historic | surprising | comforting | rewarding | verisimilitude | truthiness | oh, it's a hate read | [fill in your own] | [fill in your own] | [fill in your own]

87

TITLE:

AUTHOR:

PUB DATE: **FORMAT:**

PUBLISHER:

WHERE TO SHELVE:

START:	NOTES
FINISH:	

visual matrix

sexy | smoochy | creepy | scary | literary | explodey | funny | clever | pacing | character | originality | speculative | historic | surprising | comforting | rewarding | verisimilitude | truthiness | oh, it's a hate read | [fill in your own] | [fill in your own] | [fill in your own]

88

TITLE:

AUTHOR:

PUB DATE: **FORMAT:**

PUBLISHER:

WHERE TO SHELVE:

START:	NOTES
FINISH:	

visual matrix

sexy / smoochy / creepy / scary / literary / explodey / funny / clever / pacing / character / originality / speculative / historic / surprising / comforting / rewarding / verisimilitude / truthiness / oh, it's a hate read / [fill in your own] / [fill in your own] / [fill in your own]

89

TITLE:

AUTHOR:

PUB DATE: **FORMAT:**

PUBLISHER:

WHERE TO SHELVE:

| **START:** | NOTES |
| **FINISH:** | |

visual matrix

sexy / smoochy / creepy / scary / literary / explodey / funny / clever / pacing / character / originality / speculative / historic / surprising / comforting / rewarding / verisimilitude / truthiness / oh, it's a hate read / [fill in your own] / [fill in your own] / [fill in your own]

90

TITLE:

AUTHOR:

PUB DATE: **FORMAT:**

PUBLISHER:

WHERE TO SHELVE:

START: NOTES

FINISH:

---

visual matrix

sexy / smoochy / creepy / scary / literary / explodey / funny / clever / pacing / character / originality / speculative / historic / surprising / comforting / rewarding / verisimilitude / truthiness / oh, it's a hate read / [fill in your own] / [fill in your own] / [fill in your own]

91

TITLE:

AUTHOR:

PUB DATE: **FORMAT:**

PUBLISHER:

WHERE TO SHELVE:

| **START:** | NOTES |
| **FINISH:** | |

visual matrix

sexy / smoochy / creepy / scary / literary / explodey / funny / clever / pacing / character / originality / speculative / historic / surprising / comforting / rewarding / verisimilitude / truthiness / oh, it's a hate read / [fill in your own] / [fill in your own] / [fill in your own]

TITLE:

AUTHOR:

PUB DATE: **FORMAT:**

PUBLISHER:

WHERE TO SHELVE:

START: NOTES

FINISH:

visual matrix

| sexy | smoochy | creepy | scary | literary | explodey | funny | clever | pacing | character | originality | speculative | historic | surprising | comforting | rewarding | verisimilitude | truthiness | oh, it's a hate read | [fill in your own] | [fill in your own] | [fill in your own] |

TITLE:

AUTHOR:

PUB DATE: **FORMAT:**

PUBLISHER:

WHERE TO SHELVE:

START:	NOTES
FINISH:	

visual matrix

sexy | smoochy | creepy | scary | literary | explodey | funny | clever | pacing | character | originality | speculative | historic | surprising | comforting | rewarding | verisimilitude | truthiness | oh, it's a hate read | [fill in your own] | [fill in your own] | [fill in your own]

TITLE:

AUTHOR:

PUB DATE: **FORMAT:**

PUBLISHER:

WHERE TO SHELVE:

START: NOTES

FINISH:

---

visual matrix

sexy / smoochy / creepy / scary / literary / explodey / funny / clever / pacing / character / originality / speculative / historic / surprising / comforting / rewarding / verisimilitude / truthiness / oh, it's a hate read / [fill in your own] / [fill in your own] / [fill in your own]

TITLE:

AUTHOR:

PUB DATE: **FORMAT:**

PUBLISHER:

WHERE TO SHELVE:

START:	NOTES
FINISH:	

visual matrix

sexy · smoochy · creepy · scary · literary · explodey · funny · clever · pacing · character · originality · speculative · historic · surprising · comforting · rewarding · verisimilitude · truthiness · oh, it's a hate read · [fill in your own] · [fill in your own] · [fill in your own]

96

TITLE:

AUTHOR:

PUB DATE: **FORMAT:**

PUBLISHER:

WHERE TO SHELVE:

START: NOTES

FINISH:

---

visual matrix

sexy · smoochy · creepy · scary · literary · explodey · funny · clever · pacing · character · originality · speculative · historic · surprising · comforting · rewarding · verisimilitude · truthiness · oh, it's a hate read · [fill in your own] · [fill in your own] · [fill in your own]

97

TITLE:

AUTHOR:

PUB DATE: **FORMAT:**

PUBLISHER:

WHERE TO SHELVE:

START:	NOTES
FINISH:	

visual matrix

sexy | smoochy | creepy | scary | literary | explodey | funny | clever | pacing | character | originality | speculative | historic | surprising | comforting | rewarding | verisimilitude | truthiness | oh, it's a hate read | [fill in your own] | [fill in your own] | [fill in your own]

TITLE:

AUTHOR:

PUB DATE: **FORMAT:**

PUBLISHER:

WHERE TO SHELVE:

START: NOTES

FINISH:

visual matrix

sexy | smoochy | creepy | scary | literary | explodey | funny | clever | pacing | character | originality | speculative | historic | surprising | comforting | rewarding | verisimilitude | truthiness | oh, it's a hate read | [fill in your own] | [fill in your own] | [fill in your own]

TITLE:

AUTHOR:

PUB DATE: **FORMAT:**

PUBLISHER:

WHERE TO SHELVE:

START: NOTES

FINISH:

---

visual matrix

| sexy | smoochy | creepy | scary | literary | explodey | funny | clever | pacing | character | originality | speculative | historic | surprising | comforting | rewarding | verisimilitude | truthiness | oh, it's a hate read | [fill in your own] | [fill in your own] | [fill in your own] |

100

TITLE:

AUTHOR:

PUB DATE: **FORMAT:**

PUBLISHER:

WHERE TO SHELVE:

| **START:** | NOTES |
| **FINISH:** | |

visual matrix

sexy / smoochy / creepy / scary / literary / explodey / funny / clever / pacing / character / originality / speculative / historic / surprising / comforting / rewarding / verisimilitude / truthiness / oh, it's a hate read / [fill in your own] / [fill in your own] / [fill in your own]

TITLE:

AUTHOR:

PUB DATE: **FORMAT:**

PUBLISHER:

WHERE TO SHELVE:

START: NOTES

FINISH:

---

visual matrix

| sexy | smoochy | creepy | scary | literary | explodey | funny | clever | pacing | character | originality | speculative | historic | surprising | comforting | rewarding | verisimilitude | truthiness | oh, it's a hate read | [fill in your own] | [fill in your own] | [fill in your own] |

TITLE:

AUTHOR:

PUB DATE: **FORMAT:**

PUBLISHER:

WHERE TO SHELVE:

START: NOTES

FINISH:

---

visual matrix

sexy | smoochy | creepy | scary | literary | explodey | funny | clever | pacing | character | originality | speculative | historic | surprising | comforting | rewarding | verisimilitude | truthiness | oh, it's a hate read | [fill in your own] | [fill in your own] | [fill in your own]

TITLE:

AUTHOR:

PUB DATE: **FORMAT:**

PUBLISHER:

WHERE TO SHELVE:

START: NOTES

FINISH:

visual matrix

sexy / smoochy / creepy / scary / literary / explodey / funny / clever / pacing / character / originality / speculative / historic / surprising / comforting / rewarding / verisimilitude / truthiness / oh, it's a hate read / [fill in your own] / [fill in your own] / [fill in your own]

TITLE:

AUTHOR:

PUB DATE: **FORMAT:**

PUBLISHER:

WHERE TO SHELVE:

START: NOTES

FINISH:

visual matrix

sexy / smoochy / creepy / scary / literary / explodey / funny / clever / pacing / character / originality / speculative / historic / surprising / comforting / rewarding / verisimilitude / truthiness / oh, it's a hate read / [fill in your own] / [fill in your own] / [fill in your own]

TITLE:

AUTHOR:

PUB DATE: **FORMAT:**

PUBLISHER:

WHERE TO SHELVE:

START:	NOTES
FINISH:	

visual matrix

sexy | smoochy | creepy | scary | literary | explodey | funny | clever | pacing | character | originality | speculative | historic | surprising | comforting | rewarding | verisimilitude | truthiness | oh, it's a hate read | [fill in your own] | [fill in your own] | [fill in your own]

TITLE:

AUTHOR:

PUB DATE: **FORMAT:**

PUBLISHER:

WHERE TO SHELVE:

START:	NOTES
FINISH:	

visual matrix

sexy / smoochy / creepy / scary / literary / explodey / funny / clever / pacing / character / originality / speculative / historic / surprising / comforting / rewarding / verisimilitude / truthiness / oh, it's a hate read / [fill in your own] / [fill in your own] / [fill in your own]

TITLE:

AUTHOR:

PUB DATE: **FORMAT:**

PUBLISHER:

WHERE TO SHELVE:

START:	NOTES
FINISH:	

visual matrix

sexy | smoochy | creepy | scary | literary | explodey | funny | clever | pacing | character | originality | speculative | historic | surprising | comforting | rewarding | verisimilitude | truthiness | oh, it's a hate read | [fill in your own] | [fill in your own] | [fill in your own]

108

TITLE:

AUTHOR:

PUB DATE: **FORMAT:**

PUBLISHER:

WHERE TO SHELVE:

START: NOTES

FINISH:

visual matrix

sexy / smoochy / creepy / scary / literary / explodey / funny / clever / pacing / character / originality / speculative / historic / surprising / comforting / rewarding / verisimilitude / truthiness / oh, it's a hate read / [fill in your own] / [fill in your own] / [fill in your own]

109

TITLE:

AUTHOR:

PUB DATE: **FORMAT:**

PUBLISHER:

WHERE TO SHELVE:

START:	NOTES
FINISH:	

visual matrix

sexy / smoochy / creepy / scary / literary / explodey / funny / clever / pacing / character / originality / speculative / historic / surprising / comforting / rewarding / verisimilitude / truthiness / oh, it's a hate read / [fill in your own] / [fill in your own] / [fill in your own]

TITLE:

AUTHOR:

PUB DATE: **FORMAT:**

PUBLISHER:

WHERE TO SHELVE:

START: NOTES

FINISH:

visual matrix

sexy | smoochy | creepy | scary | literary | explodey | funny | clever | pacing | character | originality | speculative | historic | surprising | comforting | rewarding | verisimilitude | truthiness | oh, it's a hate read | [fill in your own] | [fill in your own] | [fill in your own]

TITLE:

AUTHOR:

PUB DATE: **FORMAT:**

PUBLISHER:

WHERE TO SHELVE:

START: NOTES

FINISH:

---

visual matrix

sexy | smoochy | creepy | scary | literary | explodey | funny | clever | pacing | character | originality | speculative | historic | surprising | comforting | rewarding | verisimilitude | truthiness | oh, it's a hate read | [fill in your own] | [fill in your own] | [fill in your own]

112

TITLE:

AUTHOR:

PUB DATE: **FORMAT:**

PUBLISHER:

WHERE TO SHELVE:

START:	NOTES
FINISH:	

visual matrix

sexy | smoochy | creepy | scary | literary | explodey | funny | clever | pacing | character | originality | speculative | historic | surprising | comforting | rewarding | verisimilitude | truthiness | oh, it's a hate read | [fill in your own] | [fill in your own] | [fill in your own]

TITLE:

AUTHOR:

PUB DATE: **FORMAT:**

PUBLISHER:

WHERE TO SHELVE:

START:	NOTES
FINISH:	

visual matrix

| sexy | smoochy | creepy | scary | literary | explodey | funny | clever | pacing | character | originality | speculative | historic | surprising | comforting | rewarding | verisimilitude | truthiness | oh, it's a hate read | [fill in your own] | [fill in your own] | [fill in your own] |

TITLE:

AUTHOR:

PUB DATE: **FORMAT:**

PUBLISHER:

WHERE TO SHELVE:

START:	NOTES
FINISH:	

visual matrix

sexy | smoochy | creepy | scary | literary | explodey | funny | clever | pacing | character | originality | speculative | historic | surprising | comforting | rewarding | verisimilitude | truthiness | oh, it's a hate read | [fill in your own] | [fill in your own] | [fill in your own]

TITLE:

AUTHOR:

PUB DATE: **FORMAT:**

PUBLISHER:

WHERE TO SHELVE:

START:	NOTES
FINISH:	

visual matrix

sexy / smoochy / creepy / scary / literary / explodey / funny / clever / pacing / character / originality / speculative / historic / surprising / comforting / rewarding / verisimilitude / truthiness / oh, it's a hate read / [fill in your own] / [fill in your own] / [fill in your own]

THE
LISTS

GENRE

GENRE

GENRE

GENRE

GENRE

118

GENRE

GENRE

GENRE

GENRE

GENRE

GENRE

GENRE

GENRE

GENRE

GENRE

www.ingramcontent.com/pod-product-compliance
Lightning Source LLC
Chambersburg PA
CBHW060532080526
44586CB00012B/713